Beckmann Variations
& other poems

Michael Heller is a poet, essayist and critic. Among his recent books are *Eschaton, Two Novellas: Marble Snows and The Study* and *Speaking the Estranged: Essays on the Work of George Oppen*. He wrote the libretto for the recently performed opera, *Benjamin*, based on the life of Walter Benjamin. His awards include the NEH Poet/Scholar grant, the Di Castagnola Prize and New York Foundation for the Arts Fellowships. He was born in 1937 in New York City, where he now lives.

Also by Michael Heller

Poetry
Two Poems
Accidental Center
Knowledge
Figures Of Speaking
In The Builded Place
Marginalia In A Desperate Hand
Wordflow
Exigent Futures: New and Selected Poems
A Look At The Door With The Hinges Off
Eschaton

Prose
Earth and Cave
Living Root: A Memoir
Two Novellas: Marble Snows & The Study

Essays
Conviction's Net Of Branches:
        Essays on the Objectivist Poets and Poetry
Uncertain Poetries: Essays on Poets, Poetry and Poetics
Speaking the Estranged: Essays on the Work of George Oppen

Editor
Carl Rakosi: Man and Poet
Poets Poems #21

Beckmann Variations

& other poems

MICHAEL HELLER

Shearsman Books

Exeter

Published in the United Kingdom in 2010 by
Shearsman Books Ltd
58 Velwell Road
Exeter EX4 4LD

www.shearsman.com

ISBN 978-1-84861-087-3
First Edition

Acknowledgements

My deepest thanks to Barbara Buenger, Beckmann scholar and
editor of *Max Beckmann: Self-Portrait in Words: Collected Writings and
Statements, 1903–1950*, whose intelligence, kindness and friendship
have guided me through the writing of this work.

A portion of this work in slightly altered form was originally pub-
lished in *New England Review.* I am grateful for its appearance there.
"Notes: R.B. Kitaj at Marlborough" in *Jewish Quarterly.*
"Within the Open Landscapes" in *Poetry Salzburg Review.*
"Capriccio with Obelisk" at www.culturalsociety.org, the web site
of The Cultural Society.

For JA

Contents

Beckmann Variations

1.

Hard to forget that London morning in the winter of 2003 when my wife and I stepped on to the Number 4 bus to visit the Beckmann exhibition at the Tate Modern. We sat almost like little gods on the upper level of the bus looking down into the busy streets, watching the sere of neighborhoods change. From the north side of London, from Islington, past Angel with its milling young people, an animate sea washed against leafy Clerkenwell, ebbing and swelling around the new Sadlers Wells, the dingy newspaper offices and paper makers. And there we were, high up, going by the pubs we'd sat in and read poetry to others in. So much looked sweet and pleasant in that gritty London way. Then came the creaking turn on south to the river, a blinding arc of sun in our faces as though reality had suddenly struck out at us. Now the City lay there in all its criss-crossed busyness as did the old dilapidated East End. And finally we came to the area around St. Paul's awash in its grim English history, the Tower, Execution Dock, the rusted cages at Wapping, the Isle of Dogs. Here, where the Thames bulges north and makes a curve, the old cathedral dominates, towering over the streets, and on its grassy island, the great rain-stained edifice is docked like a battleship howsered to old England and ancient, supernatural Europe. Many years ago, I'd walked around in St. Paul's, breathing in the smoky air from the stands of burning candles, the soot blackening the paintings of Christian martyrs and saints, its spot-lit altar, a delusion or paradisical offering seen from afar over the rows of chairs that filled the floor.

But it is a short walk from St. Paul's to the Embankment and across the spidery post-modern Millennium footbridge to the South Bank and the Tate Modern with its disused brick smokestacks. I recall, on that cool morning, the two of us, walking hand-in-hand across its slim white arc. The river breezes rippled the Thames. Bright sunlight dazzled the old trim of buildings lining the banks and caught the glass windows of that architectural comedy of an office building, the Gherkin, down near Docklands. And there was a feeling in me that we were passing through ourselves, out beyond the skin and into a flow bearing our history and culture and all its entrainments, even our companionship and years of talk. That walk across the bridge, then, was part of a meditation, not only because we had so often spoken in the same breath about art and poetry but also because there were times it seemed when pictures and words so reflect on each other that they offer a powerful illumination of the world we walk through. And I thought then not only of Beckmann, whose terrifying late work I barely knew but also of Yeats, speaking to "Maurice," Maud Gonne's daughter Iseult, in *Per Amica Silentia Lunae*, telling her that he wanted to put down all things he said and had wanted to say on that day they walked together.

2. SPACE

Reise auf dem Fisch (Mann und Frau)
(Journey on the Fish [Man and Woman]), 1934

We had seen the blue spun with thin white webs
of contrails left by jets out of Heathrow,
had hoped for the promise of an infinity

that would leave a foreground for the finite,
for the savor of bodies in a room, for memory
and for this present, an entwine of emotion

and object such that its simplicity would shame
unless met head-on, as one would meet an offered glass
of wine lifted in salute, the taste of bread and butter.

Not perfection, but their transitory being in the world
to be shared with others. And so we looked up to see
how wind blew the chalky lines left by the planes

into blowsy arcs, watched the waves' ruffles as they
moved down the brown expanse of the Thames,
flowing toward Whitehall and the towers of Parliament.

It was as though we were striving against a power
impacted in those buildings. And then, in the painting,
we saw the man and woman bound by silken sashes
to the backs of fish, the waves' surfaces to be breached.

And who now could live only by a word or by an image;
who could stand back, look and speak, only to fall silent?
Who, in these times, did not sense death and non-being
as a shadow, something brushed against the cranial wall?

The bound lovers in their journey are plunged downward
and must embrace fear, rapture, the throes of love, their lips
clamped shut against the pressure. Great silvery fish sound
the ocean's deeps and seed the darkness with their silence.

If you wish to get hold of the invisible, wrote Beckmann,
you must penetrate as deeply as possible into the visible.

Space is the infinite deity.

3. Entartete Kunst

. . . the term stands for degenerate art, but "entartet" which has traditionally been translated as "degenerate" or "decadent" is essentially a biological term, defining a plant or animal that has so changed that it no longer belongs to its species. By extension, it refers to art that is unclassifiable or so far beyond the confines of what is accepted that it is in essence 'non-art.'—from the catalog for the Smithsonian's "Degenerate Art" exhibition which replicated the Nazis' Entartete Kunst of 1937. . .

Beckmann's work, along with that of most of Germany's modernist masters, was included in the Nazis' display of "degenerate art," the "Entartete Kunst" exhibition held in Munich in July of 1937. It was then that the category of "art" fell prey to the Nazi logic found in their eugenic doctrines concerning "degenerate" Jews, homosexuals, the mentally impaired. The night before the exhibition was to open, Hitler made a speech to the nation about this un-German art. Beckmann heard the broadcast, packed his belongings and with his wife fled Germany the next morning, never to return.

But there was an unintended double irony in the usage of "entartet" by the Nazis. Most serious and important art often changes in such a way that it only nominally belongs to the species it came from. Beckmann's work was "entartete," only distantly related to the flora or fauna of pictures then existing; it was already a rebuke to the art culture in which it had been created.

Beckmann's genius involves a remarkable and unsettling simultaneity of the contemporary and the archaic. In his notes, he writes of the "last days of drowned continents," of art seeking a new, evolving consciousness. The flood is part biblical, part Jungian. Beckmann's imagery is cluttered with flotsam, a detritus of objects that jar anachronistically against each other. Ancient ritual swords and modern torture machines, the kind found in the cellars of the Nazis or indeed the palaces of Saddam, co-exist on the same rectangle of canvas. Vicious plant life populates the landscape, and lovely eroticized bodies suffer excruciating cruelties. Hyperbolic realism and fantasy co-exist, held together by powerful compositional skills.

And Beckmann can deploy a remarkable sense of color and line to reinforce the drama, as with the slate greens and blacks of his early *The Sinking of the Titanic*. Here, Beckmann's unique strokes of color make the waves look less like water than like stony altar pieces on which the hapless, drowning victims are sacrificed to the new, heartless gods of modernity. The night sky above this scene of misfortune is rendered in the fiery reds of the burning ship as though it were simply another morphing of implacable malevolence.

The figures of fish, man and woman, in his painting *Journey on the Fish*, refer to the Babylonian fertility god, Ones-Dagon, part man and part aquatic animal. In Babylonian mythology, Dagon brings culture and civilization to the crude, animalistic Babylonians. He is a savage yet saving god.

But Beckmann also had before him the Great War, its "last days" offering up a continent drowned not in water but in blood. Beckmann, born in 1884, was a medical orderly on the Belgian front where he experienced first hand the disaster's physical and human rubble. Its horrors led not only to a nervous breakdown but found their way permanently into his work. The faces, the flayed and torn bodies, the clutter of ominous ritualized objects of warfare were a response, he wrote, "to an infinite space, which one must constantly pile with any kind of junk, so that one will not see behind it the terrible depth." For Beckmann, that "terrible depth" is the very space of the human arena, a seething ground of aggression and passion, iron-bound into the symbology of religion and culture but, ultimately, a place not susceptible to the curbs of reason.

Initially a patriotic even enthusiastic participant in the German cause, Beckmann, after his breakdown, came away chastened by his time on the front. The landscape of war, he wrote, was a "horror vacuii," a "depopulated sublime," a "black hole." It had produced in him an unbearable aloneness, a "boundless forsaken eternity."

This was not new, the warring men, the atrocities or mass murder of civilian populations who had at one time been put to the sword and were now bombarded or burnt alive in their homes or churches. No, the shedding of innocent blood was not new, nor was the originality of Beckmann's "entartet" creations born alone out of the unprecedented scale of the slaughter he witnessed. Yes, these same horrors saturate the work of Beckmann's contemporaries such as George Grosz and Otto Dix. And they can be found, though highly complex and distorted, in Beckmann's *Hell*, a series of eleven lithographs depicting a society gone mad with authoritarian order, lust, venality and envy. Already, in this series, where satiric commentary is dropped for a kind of investigative graphics, Beckmann's oeuvre had become "entartet." Suddenly, societal relations are depicted as spatial and juxtapositional forces. Everything shown is both villainous and hopeful, and totally interdependent. Take one element away, say the torturer and his knife in *The Night* (number 6 in the series), and the composition collapses. The "entartet" work, whether the creation of Nazi ideology and violence or of Beckmann's disturbing reconstructions of the visual field, touch the bottom of what it means to be human. Their message is overwhelming: there is nothing to be removed that will make things right.

We cannot say for sure what drove Beckmann. Possibly, coming to this "entartet" vision produced a change of heart, something of a refutation of the patriotism and theomorphic spirit that had enabled nation-building, war and conquest for thousands of years. His "eternity," he wrote, had become an "unending void." Simone Weil, in her essay on the *Iliad*, "The Poem of Force," sees in Homer's poem the inklings of the disgust and horror Beckmann felt after his experiences in the Great War. At the very least, Beckmann participates in a kind of aesthetic stoicism, transmuting his disgust and pessimism into craft. "I don't cry," he writes, "I hate tears, they are a sign of slavery. I keep my mind on my business—on a leg or an arm, on the penetration of surface." And, in a way, Beckmann's contemporary in the shift of consciousness is Goya, whose *Capriccios* and *Disasters of the War* are "entartet" with the work of painters of his time.

4.

For his part, Yeats sought, like Beckmann, to make a religion of his own rebirth. Both artists are united by their deep interest in theosophy, in Blavatsky, and in imagining, as Yeats wrote, "the dead as source of all instinct." A new strength came to Yeats in his late fifties; it contained the "pride of the adept . . . added to the pride of the artist." Proper to be wary of such strength, for the power of the occult, as Merleau-Ponty reminds us, is primarily unearned. The "occult object" is often merely a kind of privileged "ready-made," supposedly loaded with supernatural powers like a lucky charm or amulet.

But Yeats and Beckmann were first of all craftsmen, their development connected not only to the materials they worked with but to the explorations they made of their own thoughts and psychology. In *Per Amica*, Yeats cites approvingly a critic who insists that "learning to know one's own mind, gradually getting the disorder of one's mind in order, led to the real impulse to create."

For Yeats, then, there was an ethics of technique, indissolubly wed to his spiritual path. Thus he could think Wordsworth a great poet but "so often flat and heavy *partly because his moral sense, being a discipline he had not created, [was] a mere obedience."*

And isn't it a fact that this "mere obedience" exists today among many artists and poets, a creation of movements and cliques, each with their dogmas and proscriptions? Possibly Yeats would see some of the poets of today as in the company of Wordsworth, knowing only by a kind of hearsay about the tremendous struggles for the practices they employed. The poems they write would have a marvelous proficiency, a technical expertise often brilliant but seemingly brittle and unmoving. For they would have acquired their means as though by birthright, as though the forms into which opinion suggests they cast their work are already occult "ready-mades," approved by their peers and the community of scholars whose approval they sought. By this, the power of their poetry would be vitiated, made a null in the poet's intercourse with the surrounding world. Blake, in his call not for generation but regeneration, had said it: to be reborn is always more important than to be born.

A graph of Beckmann's struggle, the war for his state of mind, can be tracked in the self-portraits, master works of that genre, as Beckmann seems to surrender his own psychic health to the "depths" he insisted on depicting. His vulnerabilities are poignantly displayed in the 1917 *Self Portrait with Red Scarf*, painted after his breakdown. A tense, haggard Beckmann is pinioned at the window of his studio, his right arm pushing against the picture frame, the left bent at the elbow in a ninety-degree angle that mimics the entrapping, boxed-in effect of the lower right side corner of the canvas. The mood is claustrophobic. The eyes look away, averted from the painting on the easel, watching for what catastrophe approaches in the distance. In later self-portraits, particularly those of the twenties, Beckmann often scowls. Whether surrounded by the tools of his trade or by musical instruments (he loved American jazz), he expresses a wary vigilance against art as any kind of deliverance. By the early thirties, when Beckmann had achieved both critical and financial success, the self-portraits, especially the brazen bull-shaped figure of Beckmann in his tuxedo, radiate a complex self-confidence that borders on the arrogance of one who has seen it all and finds the 'game' of art and even society utterly distasteful.

Beckmann envisioned his art as a spiritual quest. His studio in Amsterdam (where he had fled after Hitler's speech), an old tobacco warehouse, was filled, he claimed, "with figures from the old days and the new, like an ocean moved by storm and sun, and always present in my thoughts." To make something of these figures, to create, had a religious cast. Beckmann was playing at god, but without a handbook of rules and injunctions. In his notebook he tells us that "the shapes" he conjured in his studio "become beings and seem comprehensible to me in the great void and uncertainty I call God."

5. ONCE THE AZTECS

Traum von Monte Carlo (Dream of Monte Carlo), 1940–1943

Once the Aztecs learned to propitiate the gods
by sacrifice, they took no risks that the sun might
rise and offered it many hearts each morning.

Thus we understood why waiters with swords
surrounded the casino's gaming tables, and why
a young actor dressed in the robes of a king stabbed

himself in the heart for the amusement of gamblers.
The great bird of Chance, whose immense wings
give it range over all of life, was caged only by a flimsy

barricade of musical instruments, horns, piccolos, the
dismembered arms of other entertainers. The lost, who
in desperation broke the rules or reached too far, found

themselves the old bird's prey. *Deus Absconditus*
had returned to judge but found himself eclipsed
in mercy for those who made obeisance to their hopes.

6.

Yeats speaks of man and his daimon as being fundamentally severed, but in our age it is only fundamentalists who have been able to keep that separation. Our time has collapsed the old orders, and man and his word, while not One, are, strangely, not two either. There is always dissonance, and those who make to harmonize it, or explain it away as illusion, only set the problem back farther. This dissonance here ringing through the world set me to talk about paintings.

But first, when the daimon and the one he or she inhabits form a bond, the old vibrancy by which a poem is illuminated is lost, even discredited. Yeats, who, along with Beckmann, backdrops this writing, says "He who keeps the distant stars within His fold comes without intermediary." A discordant sibilance holds the sentence together, for who now can keep Yeats's capital "H" in his "His," who can find beauty but in a fold of the world as profane as it is sacred? Again, the reason for turning to look at Beckmann's pictures.

Beckmann, it struck me, does not bring one back to a known world, but to a potential of the world that surrounds one. His work, rather than a comment, is an excitation (ex-citore, a calling out or summoning forth), simultaneously concrete and illusory. He is at once melodramatic and prophetic, as in the great central panel of his triptych, *Schauspieler* (Actors) of 1941–42. Here, a player, modeled perhaps after Beckmann himself, wearing the royal crown, plunges a knife into his own chest while beside him, a masked woman sings. While the blood spurts from the breast of the actor-king, the woman looks elsewhere. Her song is her part in the drama, and she will perform no matter the surrounding horrors, knife wounds or the murderous scene depicted beneath the floorboards of the stage. Her voice will stop up the screams coming from below. She will look away from the dying actor; one imagines her eyes aflutter, enwrapt in her scene. And it is a kind of truism of Beckmann's pictures: people's eyes almost never meet. The tormented figures in the pictures own their projections. They are paranoiac, and bound by the law of psychic economy to convert the motive and action of others into their own private and anguished symbol system.

Which is why, Beckmann seems to tell us, the daimon is no longer separate, no longer, as Yeats thought, a contrary of the human. Each modern soul is alone, without his "H," without the sharp transversal of values created by opposition. A terrible non-relativity pervades.

Which is also art's gap to articulate, to heal. Baudelaire, according to Wallace Stevens, "felt that there exists an unascertained and fundamental aesthetic or order, of which poetry and painting are manifestations." Stevens calls this the "constructive faculty," derived not from the sensibility but the imagination. Not ekphrasis but a kind of insolvent parallelism of gains and losses. For, at best, the poet can only hope to transfer the energy of Beckmann's work, not by describing it, but by enacting something like a Baudelairean "correspondence," making a figure that will release in *language* the power of the painting.

7. THE KING

Der König (The King), 1933, 1937

He, beside the wheel, and the shrouded counselor at his back
  must whisper.
Niobe faces away, her bent arm lies across his sex. Eyes sunk in
  shade,
gaze emanating from blackened pits. Iron chair swathed in damask.
The implements are hidden under regal blankets.

The way of kings, the way of empires.
What can I still extract from the last ruins of a royal house
—how can I still make the planetary systems tremble?

Only by this—surrender. Or enable the wheel's turn.
His subjects form a chorus; they sing hymns to vibratory
  landscapes,
to diadems of cities. Half-lidded eye under its black indenture.
The monarch looks out from that place where his powers sleep.

Kings bear the force of statuary. Statuary seals up the force of kings.

Forms' outlines make for transitory limits. Malevolence, not an act but a radiance.

8.

Beckmann insisted that he hardly needed "to abstract things, for each object is unreal enough already, so unreal that I can make it real only by means of painting." Beckmann, laying out his designs, choosing the colors and their tints, composing in the manner of Yeats's vision of the "soul," and its "plastic power," a power that can "mould it to any shape it will by an act of imagination." Beckmann working in the style of the ancients who in their soul-making, Yeats said, "offered sheaves of corn, fragrant gums, and the odor of fruit and flowers, *and the blood of victims.*"

Both Beckmann and Yeats sensed the soul's inexpressibility, to be approached only by successive works, by catenaries of imaginings, unending works. Yeats exclaiming "because I seek an image not a book," that the wisest men in their writings were those "who own nothing but their blind stupefied hearts." He argued against "song," against sweetness or happiness, against the artist who became a "fly in marmalade." Underneath these thoughts is a fear, one that Beckmann shared, of being trapped by harmony and beauty, being lulled into easy belief, complacency or remorse. Beckmann endlessly instructs his students: "do not try to capture nature." Beckmann's longing can only be expressed in what cannot be a copied reality. His message to the poet is that nature is mute, inarticulate. The inexpressible produces words only as irritants, words that never leave off—one never quite arrives at the inexpressible.

9. Into the Heart of the Real

Abtransport der Sphinxe (Removal of the Sphinxes), 1945

The Sphinxes have beautifully outlined breasts, and they stand proudly on their taloned feet. And their taloned feet rest proudly on stone pedestals. Wood for crates is stacked nearby, and a sister bird has taken flight. Each sphinx, from its platform, tells a seductive tale. Each one makes a liar out of one of the others. Whether on the pediments of stone or placed for shipment on the tumbrils, they insist on whispering silky words in one's ear. Little breezes are stirred by their sibilant words, little swirls that are worse than typhoons or tornadoes. Big storms, hurricanes are the exhalants of the world's turning, of massive pressure gradients at the poles, knocking down buildings and flooding streets. But the tiny voices of the sphinxes enter through the ears like silkworms; each weaves a gummy dream to the bones of the skull as though it were a shadow on the wall of Plato's cave. Each tiny voice blends in with the sound of the real, urgent, unappeasable. There's an official monitoring each skull who, even as he listens, is already insisting on the dream's removal. The sphinxes must be carted off. One thinks that the officials would organize deliveries of this nature in secret or at least elsewhere, but no, I have seen each one at the embarkation point eagerly straining on a rope, gleaming with sweat, pulling the crates toward the outgoing barges.

10.

Only the "law of discontinuity," as the German dramatist Georg Büchner named it, gives a strange coherence to the art of Beckmann. Beckmann wrote and published a number of plays that key off the emotional tonalities of Büchner's work, but that "law" is to be found most faithfully enacted in Beckmann's pictures. Scale, proportion, harmonies of palette (though he is a great colorist), these are almost totally rejected or re-invented. In this sense, the history of Beckmann's paintings nearly does not exist.

Twentieth-century German Expressionism, the movement to which Beckmann's works are often assigned, took the corrupted world of culture and society, poured vitriol and a chemical softening agent over it, and then, like a finger-painting child, smeared and pulled its visual contents into all sorts of shapes. But always, these expressionists left memory, left trace marks that led back to the world constituted in those Berlin or Viennese rooms, in coffeehouses of the city, in the world just outside its windows. They gave the viewer its night, the fouled psychic moonless night of that world. Yes, it took light away, emulating the setting and risings of the sun. Day, even if it never returned, remained a possibility.

Beckmann's major works stand outside that nostalgia. His proto-mythic worlds contain no visible pathways back to ours except through a psychic universe of pain, suffering and violence. We come into Beckmann's world via biology rather than history or memory. Anachronisms abound: modern instruments of war or torture are placed amidst settings of archaic beauty; balloons and windmills entrap figures wearing the garments of the ancients. The rhythms of his paintings, shorn of perspective or size, are not natural but musical. The viewer who would be true to Beckmann's vision cannot talk directly about his projected images; no existing discourse contains them or even echoes with them. Instead, the viewer must create a response, must confront them with an artwork, mental or actual, of his own—he must make up their story.

Which is what Beckmann himself did in relation to his world, one saturated with malevolent power and violence, violence which he experienced firsthand in the Great War. He understood that violence severed the relation between oneself and the world's objects. There was no building on such a world, not even a capacity to alter it, as he felt his fellow painters attempted in their satires and art-political parlor games. To express the transformed relationships, he must create a new world. Looked at in an art-historical context, ominousness and the ever presence of violence are, for Beckmann, the alchemist's lodestone, invoking terrible new relations. Hopeful prophecy need not apply.

The Nazis' Degenerate Art Exhibition, in which Beckmann's work figured so prominently, also illustrated an instance of discontinuity's law, atomizing two hundred years of previous German art history, not merely to turn it retroactively on its head, but to invent a National Socialist aesthetics that, like Beckmann's work, had never actually existed. It can be said that Beckmann responded in kind.

11. DEPARTURE

Abfahrt (Departure), 1932–1933

The master departs he always departs.
So it is with kings who sail off on boat-like thrones,
who perform the miracles of going. Don't wonders
occur when iron reason has left the scene,
and cruel profanations no longer astound us?

The king-drummer's beat is a ritual, an enclosing
rhythm of prisoners bound by rope. They look glum
tied in their bundles, one head up, another head down,
hair brushing the same ground on which we place our feet.

Later, there will be torture, but for now, only your servants,
these women, relieve us of slaughter. We embody the gift
of powerlessness. The king sails off, his spirit dispersed
among the males. He sails off, his spirit dispersed among us.

The last lines of "Departure" are not statements about masculine and feminine energy states. Rather they depict the contradictions within role models as Beckmann saw them, men because of their physical strength pressed into violence, women as reluctant sirens of force and power. But in the kingdom, wherever choices exist, there is always terror, fomented by one's relation to state or cultural power, to orders of belonging and not belonging, along with concomitant penalties for transgression.

And yet, as seen across history, the fear of the tyrant is only exceeded by the fear of not having one. For the tyrant can set all things "right"; he can transgress the law while embodying it. Beckmann shows this embodiment with all its emotional coloration at the moment of regal abandonment. The master departs or merely sleeps while others in the bureaucracy enforce the power of his rule—and so every step of distancing or departure solidifies the master's power. For his subjects, departure is not an opportunity to find freedom but to experience loss.

Under this ruler, all language is decree, and only the operations of the poet might undo the law.

12. LOOKING WARILY

Selbstbildnis mit Trompete (Self-Portrait with Horn), 1938

at the horn, the fullness of its bell is blocked by the doorframe as the completeness of the man is blocked by the edge of the picture frame as the fullness of the note that might issue from the horn is blocked as the artist has averted his lips from the mouthpiece as his left hand has an uncertain grasp on the horn's metal as his right hand is poised to catch the horn if it falls as his left hand is his right hand and his right hand his left as the doorframe is really the frame about a mirror as the eyes look at the horn with animus as anyone can see the mirror is tilted at an angle such that if it were a real mirror and not a mirror in a painting but real on a real wall it would not reflect back the image of the viewer.

13.

Complexity, or life bending and modifying within the known. Possible that the artist's clarity can complicate reality. With the sphinxes gone, the secret murmurings about the real are silenced by rationality and official injunction. The artist-individual is left to realize the story as chimera, as *para-* or *as-if*. As temporary. Truth can live for a short time, if not within ourselves at least within the minds of others.

Both Beckmann and Yeats had personal encounters with William Blake. Beckmann went so far as to have a conversation with him in which Blake counseled "Have faith in objects. Do not let yourself be intimidated by the horror of the world. Everything is ordered and right and must fulfill its destiny in order to obtain perfection. Seek this path and you will obtain from your own self even deeper perception of the eternal beauty of creation; you will attain increasing release from all that which now seems to you sad or terrible."

Beckmann's world teeters on the edge of such realization. Its values inverted. Force muffles loss, and the artist must work another way, by depicting power. Power is created by those who, in their psychic construction, are other than ourselves. The collective may be the first expression of power but not its first cause. Beckmann's paintings, through their sensual appeals and absorbing surface textures, show the madness of power but also lead us to the very lineaments of desire that might overthrow power. As in Blake, Beckmann's visions expose the energy from which power arises, but also show how that energy undermines destructive force. His paintings present not so much illusionistic difficulties as an overarching undecidability concerning how to decipher their private codes and symbols. In this, Beckmann, again, resembles the Blake of the Prophetic Books and the Yeats of the Golden Dawn as well. What they create arrives, as Yeats said of his poetry, out of the "general cistern of form."

Neoplatonism, not as a theo-philosophic religion but as a generational tie, creating a sense that, as the painter and the poet demonstrate, prophecy is the first fruit of history, but history is also the first fruit of prophecy.

14. ORDERS

Luftballon mit Windmühle (Balloon with Windmill). 1947

The order of the profane assists the coming of
a messianic kingdom, despoiled of gods.

No act of the saint equals autumn's rotting leaves.
No autumn compares to lovers trapped in their cage

nor to the tutored souls lashed to the vanes of turning windmills.
All circle between heaven and hell.

The air transmits their stories, their cries.

But the background is as of the immemorial sea—flecked black
    waves,
tinged by green, globe encircling, enframing the lawful and the
    boundless.

15.

Yeats's mask knits the individual with his daimon. But the mask not only conceals the features, it also constrains the perceptions of its wearer. Its narrow eye slits and the strings that bind the mask to the forehead and ear delimit the wearer's view of reality, cut off ambient space and muffle sound. Reality is sieved through eye and nose piece. But then, what does any work of art do but create a filter? While I am absorbed in Beckmann's early masterpiece from 1912, *Untergang der Titanic (The Sinking of the Titanic)* and struggle with the pathos of the survivors milling about on the rocky ledges of the waves, I am self-blocked from a world ticking away where towers fall and armies make bloody sweeps across ancient lands. The first rule of art is fascination—and maybe its last rule as well. Everything in between is distraction, whether ideas about 'art' or genre or about the politics and social environments of the work. There is, Yeats tells us, a "deep enmity between a man and his destiny." We think of destiny as all that drives someone in time, a force or forces that the human being is either barely aware of or worse, mentally grasps but thinks beyond control. But art's fascination is, precisely, the lever that can throw one off the pre-ordained or programmed track.

The Austrian satirist, Karl Kraus, witnessing the same slow destruction of Europe that engulfed Beckmann, wrote that in this time "remembrance became a political activity and the myths of glory competed with the narratives of disillusionment for control of popular consciousness." He was aware that the Nazis had invented as a fascist myth a glorified remembrance of a world and time that never actually happened. Beckmann had lost faith with both memory and disillusion; he had opted out of the narrative game by creating a series of autarchic images. Viewers reached for them with the same desperate hopes Beckmann depicted in those passengers from the *Titanic* swimming toward the rocklike waves.

16. FALLING MAN

Abstürzender (Falling Man), 1950

It is great to fall, it will be important if I plunge
this way, as it would not be great to be entangled.

But if I plunge head down, feet clear and don't catch
on a building ledge, I will swoop past the structure

blazing in flames on my right, go past the open window
to my left where one sees some compact of love, violent

and contorted, acted out. I admit, it is great to fall, great
not to fear snagging on the buildings to the right or to the left,

wonderful to fall free from clouds swirled in turbulence,
passing toward the blue of the sea where a small boat sails,

where gulls fly like avenging angels, and the momentous inevitable
wheel of life and death has a benign dusty shine. I am going down,

dropping toward the cannibal plants, the cacti and venus fly-traps, unnameable greens and jaundiced yellows. Down.

Beckmann's *Abstürzender (Falling Man)* struck me as an image of pathos, suffused with the knowledge that an artist's work is a noticing rather than an action that can promise immediate results. This painting, among Beckmann's very last and so appearing near the end of the exhibition we had walked through, boded both dread and hope. This was my impression at least, on the day we crossed back over the bridge together to London's north side. We were unusually silent, and did not really converse again until we had boarded one of those cheery red No. 5 buses heading toward Angel.

Fallen Man. It was hard to shake the image. Beckmann's prescience or my own deeply lodged psychic imprints revived in my mind the photos from September 11th, 2001, of people who had flung themselves downward from the World Trade Center towers. And only two years after we saw the Beckmanns, young men on a suicide mission, possibly in the name of religion, exploded bombs in the London Underground on the very day we were flying from New York to Heathrow to visit our friends in Islington. They told us that one bomber had blown himself up on the No. 30 bus, the one we had often taken that wound its way down into the heart of Bloomsbury. These events drove my thoughts violently back to our trip to the Tate. They reminded me that seventeenth-century St. Paul's and the twenty-first-century Beckmann exhibition both contain paintings of spiritual significance, that both display religious-seeming triptychs, art works which had made our walk over the bridge ironically an arc across the human condition. And in our war- and atrocity-ridden time, the journey seemed entirely one way, towards Beckmann.

17. Triptych

Argonauten (The Argonauts), 1949-50

The Wall It Will Hang On

He was born Diomedes, but a centaur renamed him,
so then he was Jason to Pelias, the king who feared him
because, as Pelias's dreams warned, beware the one who
wears only one sandal, and this is how Jason came to court.

And Pelias, rather than kill the young Jason on the spot
(the boy's relatives were in attendance), said to him "Go
to Colchis for the ram's fleece." Pelias knew those masses
of gold curls were guarded by a monster who never sleeps.

Pelias was also haunted by Phrixus's ghost. Poor Phrixus
rode the wild ram to escape being made human sacrifice
by Orchomenes. Poor, dishonored Phrixus. When he died,
his corpse lay unburied, its ghost yearning for its body.

To lift the curse this deed cast, Pelias needed corpse and fleece.
And if by chance, Jason succeeded . . . well, it would go well
for Pelias either way. So Jason built the Argo. His crew,
those heroes who would later spawn a thousand myths.

Also he took on board women. Among them, rage-carrying
     Medea
and at least one invisible, interfering goddess who whispered
into Jason's ear words about fate, honor and the glories of the
     future.

Right Panel

All we are sure of is the chorus.
No single voice can sing as loud.
Frail ones empowered—thin staves
bundled with others to gain in strength.

Now unafraid, the small-minded
utter warnings and imprecations
or make a chorus of strident music,
notes stitch honor to mass identity.

Lute, pan pipe, hidden drum, voices
erasing doubt. The songs will make
the heroes do anything, will foretell
how it ends, will say hope lies in the journey.

Left Panel

The woman (Medea?), poised with sword,
sits on the death mask of a head she has lopped off.

The bearded artist paints her as he would a violent king.

Center Panel

An old man climbs the ladder from the sea.
Jason, beautiful boy, and Orpheus, lute at rest
upon the Argo's deck, are gazing at each other.

The bird of wisdom and prey perches on Jason's wrist.
The artist's eye as if painted on the bird's head stares out
 to signify attentiveness. Jason, under an eclipsed sun

around which revolve two planets. Jason, admired
and in love. Always, the artist's eye swerves toward
nourishment. The artist's eye is looking out at us.

Frame for the Future

A chorus of lovely maidens sings to quiet the waves
to harmonize with the gods that bless such voyages.

Medea has slain artifice, must slay her children.
Jason, self-absorbed, sends off the bird

who will seek ship's passage through the rocks.
Song continues. Two panels to make us compare.

Three to arouse uncertainty. Argo: hull, mast, spar.
The canvas is its sail . . .

18. BLACK SUN

The Argonauts was Beckmann's last painting, finished the day before he died suddenly of a heart attack while walking near Central Park. Critics tend to see the picture as a kind of summation of Beckmann's art, a resolution of his themes, a belief in the power of art to expose, to explain and redeem. A great calm seems to pervade this picture. The sea, which roiled the unforgiving waves before his sinking Titanic, the same expanse of water that was ready to receive his falling man, now appears only as a miniscule square in a corner of the right-hand panel. The sword of the Medea figure is the sole hint at potential violence. For this triptych, certain forces seem to have been tamed.

And yet, the triptych form as reinvented by Beckmann also produces a disturbing effect on the viewer. In older, religious-based triptychs, such as altar pieces and the stained-glass windows of churches, the separate panels form a unity held together by faith, by a hierarchical disposition. Disparate elements are transformed into harmonies under the eye of God and reinforced by compositional sightlines, restated motifs, benevolent color schemes that, like the metal hinges often used to hold the panels together, strap the work into a "vision."

But Beckmann had turned from conventional religion, from, as he wrote, "humility before God to arrogance before God," a God who failed, he insisted, because he gave mankind no means to live in peace. Beckmann's religious fervor had turned into critique: the hope that God embodies is absent. Thus his triptychs, even one as benign-seeming as The Argonauts, do not focus on paradise nor do they enact the search for salvation. His aim, he wrote, was "to sanctify the profane."

In *The Argonauts*, the mythic tale is broken up and re-arranged, transformed almost into a cubist composition. Thus, as one traverses a Beckmann triptych, the space between the panels, the gap in which one image is given up for another, assumes a powerful importance. The eye's movement between frames strikes as a leap, not toward faith, but across an abyss. What unifies is Beckmann's "godlike" stance, what he referred to as a "transcendental objectivity" (*Transzendente Sachlichkeit*) by which the most disparate elements could co-exist within a single work. In its way, the stance is the final expression of the "arrogance" he shows toward God.

And yet these last pictures are also hopelessly human and vulnerable. The harrowing descent of *Falling Man* can be seen as a freeze-frame of the artist's journey. *The Argonauts* continues that fall, only this time—as though commenting on what mankind demands from a God—the fall is into a kind of perfection, one that could render the artist's work sterile or irrelevant. Even as the triptych projects a mood of supreme ironic distance, the viewer is, in a sense, locked out. Only the figure of a temporarily eclipsed sun in the middle panel suggests that this arrestment in an ideal world of mythos is momentary. We are perhaps cautioned not to fall for it, not to fall into it.

While working on *The Argonauts*, Beckmann read about sun-spots in the writings of Alexander von Humboldt and wrote " I never knew that the sun was dark—am very shaken." Earlier, Beckmann's dark sun swam over a war-torn mankind in *Resurrection*, his unfinished painting of 1916. Corollas of eclipsed suns, planets in concentric orbits, immense revolving wheels, these form part of his iconography. Rather than unifying objects or focal points, Beckmann's suns are like black holes sucking divine energies out of the worlds they shine on. The blocked sun and orbiting planets of the triptych belong to the same malign family of stellar objects. In the months before his death, Beckmann was also reading *Empedocles*, Hölderlin's long poem about the philosopher who leapt into the gaping ash-blackened ring of Etna's smoking crater.

19.

It strikes me that each of Beckmann's paintings—because of the intrinsic beauty of its forms, the appealing shape of objects, the lovely yet eerie skin tones of its figures, because of the implicit eroticism of his images—is prophetic in two ways. Each depiction articulates the mysterious underlying forces of violence and power propelling us toward the future, that future that followed me across the Millennium bridge. But at the same time, each insists on exposing, like a revealing garment or like a keyhole in a dark room gleaming with the bright light beyond the door, something like a vision or maybe only a slight shift of perspective that would bring out the inherent beauty and hopefulness of the world we live in.

Beckmann's paintings often form a blocky rebus of human relations, delineating power and myth, but also sexual energy and allure. They are full of visual repeats, figures, faces, a multitude of musical instruments or menacing weapons, constantly being arranged and re-arranged as though a formula for human salvation might finally be worked out. One repeat is the great wheel that appears as part of the background in Beckmann's portrait from 1937 of his beloved companion, Quappi (*Quappi with White Fur*) and then reappears in *Falling Man*. A number of critics maintain that these images are of the Buddha's sacred wheel of teachings, set in motion to reclaim the world through learning and compassion. The image obtrudes into both paintings, a strange alien object, interrupting an already unconventional narrative flow, forcing the viewer to account for it, to imagine how it is part of the story. On the bridge that day, this intrusion of the wheel into the picture seemed to interfere with the dreadful story *Fallen Man* was trying to articulate. And I wanted to say yes, to affirm that it represented both hope and succor, but, also, that it felt tangible, real, like seeing the painter's hand over the canvas as a marker against the generalized prophecy of what might come.

I remember the sage's metaphor—that we live riding on the edge of a burning razor, capable at any moment of falling into the swamps of psychosis and neurosis, of projecting our fears onto the world. Beckmann's themes are dark, but throughout there are those clusters of paint, those many affectionate pictures of Quappi, that make me think not so much of ease or contentment but of love and companionship.

20.

The other day, I had to go out of town to see a sick friend, and when I came home, there was a note from my wife beside the manuscript of this work, lying on the desk:

To M. on your Beckmann meditations.

The thing is: you want to put in everything you ever thought or said as we walked together (or keep walking) and yet, looking at Beckmann you see not everything can be there, or here, in the work. You want to be as wide as the sky and endless and open as the sky seems when we're on the arc of the bridge in the middle of the Thames—but there are limits. The painting has a frame, so the viewer can get at least some of the power that grips the painter, who's frustrated because the canvas is never big enough. He has to settle for condensation.

*

(Or is it a dialogue, and the "other" talks back? How is the painter's painting telling you something? About what you thought you thought—?

J.

Postscript:
The World As Contested Arena

I would like to emphasize that I have never been politically active in any way. I have only tried to realize my conception of the world as intensely as possible.
—from 'On My Painting' by Max Beckmann, delivered 21 July 1938, London.

One thing I did not foresee, not having the courage of my own thoughts: the growing murderousness of the world.—Yeats, 1921.

Beckmann's painting, [Tot], will not allow peaceful viewing.
—William Kentridge

21. DEAD-NESS

Tot (Death), 1938

As if days were not for sanity, we encountered a blinding centerless light, a radiant light, as from a diademed god, hungry for sacrifice, feeding on human restlessness.

Who can write out cruelty as an antidote to cruelty? Who can prophesy or conjure dream-states that resist events when only the dead can sense any ceremony in the horrific world that surrounds them?

The coiled serpent, time unto eternity, makes ready to strike. The monkey-angel, trumpet and penis erect, mocks from the ceiling over the coffined body whose last breath uttered a history that gives terror and dread their public edge.

Have you found the secret mental limb of art, the appendage that like a phantom arm or leg outlined in thick, black strokes, drags us as we move through the world?

Who will write the elegy to human powerlessness in an archaic tongue?

Between self and death, we are torn by obligations and desires to which we owe the moral duty of our fears.

22.

Beckmann's *Tot* is one of his most remarkable visions, disorienting and complex. Dating from 1938, it was painted in Amsterdam shortly after Beckmann heard Hitler's radio broadcast on Degenerate Art and fled Nazi Germany for the Netherlands, never to return to his native country.

The painting depicts a funeral rite, with a coffin and female cadaver at the center of the picture. A band of blue, like a slice of the sky, divides the picture into upper and lower horizontal areas. In the lower portion, on the left, a woman fixes her shoe while behind her a figure in an apron approaches, holding a serving tray. To their right, in the center, an attendant, raising up an unlit candle, gazes down into the coffin, perhaps having finished performing arcane ablutions and special rites to usher the dead body into the underworld. The attendant seems almost normal until one notices that there are a half-dozen splayed feet protruding from beneath the gown. At the far right, a woman copulates with a large fish. In the upper area, there are even more grotesque figures painted upside down: on the right, a monster, all teeth and jaws, snakes writhing around skulls, a repulsive winged monkey- or dog-faced angel whose erect penis and the trumpet he is blowing seem to break the picture plane. At the far right, a trio of multi-faced and tuxedo-ed figures sing from the sheet music they are holding.

Perhaps it is incorrect to suggest that these figures are suspended from the ceiling, because when I rotate the image reproduced in my catalog by 180 degrees, the upside down figures are as firmly rooted to the horizontal edge of the picture as those in the lower half. Not an object, not a hair nor any item of clothing seems subject to the pull of gravity from the lower half of the picture. Everything looks compositionally correct in its own way. Clearly, in order to execute the painting, Beckmann must have constantly taken it off the easel, rotated it until the bottom was the top and the top the bottom and then painted in the figures. This quality, almost as though gravity were abolished, leads the artist William Kentridge in his essay on *Tot* to refer to what he calls its "reversibility." Beckmann, in keeping with the theme of the title, bisects this horizontality with the corpse in the coffin laid out for burial, mouth open in the rictus of dying.

Another way to see this image, in keeping with modern theories of time and space that were coming to the fore in the early twentieth century, is to imagine the blue band running across the middle of the picture as the sky. And then to see that the upper and lower physical spaces containing the figures and objects are merely bent over each other in a kind of claustrophobic Riemannian space-warp as though the world itself were a pair of jaws, the roof and bottom of a mouth, about to clamp down on each other and crush or masticate everything in Beckmann's universe.

Kentridge, in his essay, likens the angel-monkey's trumpet to those in Michelangelo's *The Last Judgment,* the immense ceiling painting in the Sistine Chapel. If there is a connection, it may be that the hosts of Michelangelo's painting have migrated into a polyvalent space where the modern and the archaic co-exist or rather co-contend for the consciousness and soul of the viewer. Thus, to one side of the squat angel, the multi-faced singers in modern tuxedos holding their sheet-music are singing a dirge or a hallelujah, and the enormous severed head beside them, like a massive carving or Indonesian temple ruin, sprouts feet from its neck, as though about to migrate to another time. The monstrous shapes, nightmarish creatures, the teeth-filled mouths and wiggling serpents in attendance, have their ancestry in Hieronymus Bosch, one of the painters Beckmann called an "old friend." And these figures, so assuredly fixed to both the floor and the ceiling above the coffin, make one feel that Beckmann aims to show something other than the usual heaven/hell contestation. For, unlike that contrast between the paradisical and the earthly or that landscape apposition in which land and sea are either harmonized or contrasted with sky, both realms of Beckmann's picture are part of the same psychic war, unified structurally by death and the coffin.

Although in exhibits and catalogues over the years this picture has been titled *Death*, Beckmann himself, in his handwritten list of completed titles, named the painting *Tot*—dead—and not *Tod*—death. The distinction between these two terms offers a clue into further reflections about Beckmann's intentions in the work, for, in its way, the mistitled picture provides a visual register of the trauma of Beckmann's exile. Its formal qualities embody the pain of the artist's dislocation, estrangement, culture-shock and anguished disorientation. Surely Beckmann felt the numbing effects of his imposed exile. At the beginning of this period Beckmann, in his isolation, spoke mostly to the haunted voices in his new home, the tobacco loft in Amsterdam. But he did not passively succumb to that numbness, to that implosion of unexpected forces that hammer a wedge between the artist's life and his materials. Beckmann responded in a unique way. *Tot* is a record of that response. Rather than offering a contemplation on the subject of "death," the painting portrays what feeling "dead" is like for the artist. This conclusion seems obvious from the powerful energies that flow over the picture's surface, energies that seem derived from Beckmann's readings, his personal circumstances and, most importantly, the powerful techniques stemming from his learning and experience that he was able to deploy in creating his works. Beckmann's *Tot* (his "dead"—the corpse in the coffin) is as much metaphysical and psychological as physical.

During the period of *Tot*'s creation, Beckmann was reading Buddhist and Hindu texts. He found in them a series of ideas, he insisted, "that drives us along the eternal and never-ending journey we must make." The imperative tone here, hinting at a path the individual only partially chooses, reminds us that *Tot*, among its many themes, explores the painter's own sense of a personal fatalism invoked by exile and fear.

Beckmann was already aware of the psychic perils of feeling "dead" as opposed to just being dead. The Nazis frightened and inhibited him, and in a sense, they made him capable of frightening himself. Even in the early nineteen-thirties, Beckmann was undertaking an internal retreat, one that would finally lead to his actual exile. By 1934, he had become a "suspect" artist, and curators and buyers were quietly removing his work from museum and gallery collections all over Germany, often under direct pressure from National Socialist groups. His teaching jobs were threatened, and the relations with his friends and patrons, some of them Jewish, came under severe strain. Beckmann's fear for his own safety made him wary to the point of paranoia—in this case an accurate word—concerning the reception of his work. In the mid-thirties he finished his great triptych *Abfahrt (Departure)*, one of his most magnificent and powerful creations. And yet when his friends and patrons came to visit his studio, he showed them only the central panel with its "mythical" spaces of archaic figure and seascape. Superficially, this panel seemed both timeless and apolitical. The right and left panels, with their images of horror, torture and extreme physical restraint, he kept hidden, since they might well be interpreted as a statement about the Nazi regime's methods and excesses. As we know, no amount of secrecy prevented any artist from being declared "degenerate" by the regime. Beckmann's self-exile, internal and then real, must be regarded as not only a desire to find safety but as an artistic statement in itself.

Tot can be viewed as a vortex, a visual symbol of an intense and evolving combat between the deadly ideologies pressing on Beckmann and an inherent life force that pressed back. Thus, in a way that is both traditional and singular, the coffin with its dead body is the painting's primary locus, its function derived, in part, from that strain of gnostic or Buddhist thought where the hope for useful knowledge on existence lies in the gap between living states of mind. If, as Beckmann's proper title suggests, his subject is the feeling of being "dead," then coffin and body are only provisionally the aesthetic center, functioning as a point of departure. From this place, Beckmann sets out to make a journey into the complexities of his own deadness and depression, the products of his exile. In fact, any move from that point, that "dead center," leads to irresolvable conflict in that the viewer's eye, rather than being carried toward the picture's center, is drawn outward into all kinds of contradictory perspectival lines, real and implied, that move in directions back and forth across and away from the center to the divided upper and lower bands. Even at the stationary coffin, where we expect the eye to rest, a burning candle lures one's gaze away from the greenish corpse and down its length, as though giving the eye permission to veer off into the imaginary web of force-lines that pull one across the picture surface. A somatic effect ensues, a hyper-intensifying energy that enters one's psyche and transforms the cliché of a restful death into endless seizures of anxiety, despair and cruelty, as though the last moment of consciousness is still riven with agitated failures and forlornness. The picture expresses the condition of being deadened by a fury of self-cancelling vectors, inhibiting action yet still arousing trouble and anxiety.

For these reasons, this picture cannot be placed in the same genre as Velázquez's or Manet's dead figures around which there is an absolute stillness intended to bring us within the state of death itself, with its finality and total closure of human activity. Beckmann's *Tot* keeps the viewer one step back from death, from the dead figure, to make us re-experience the fear of dying, and the way it wreaks havoc in our minds, assaulting our most instinctual apparatus. For Beckmann, these experiences are the source of all the viciousness and cruelty in the world. To borrow Yeats's term, here is the "murderousness" of the world totally arrayed around us.

23.

Three-quarters of a century ago, Beckmann's paintings had begun to depict this world in a precursory fashion. Like the cubists, he began to destroy perspective, wanting the illusion of depth to be seen as symbolical rather than realistic. All objects in the depiction were now to co-exist on the same teeming psychic plane. As with the pre-Renaissance painters of religious subjects, the shape of visual reality in Beckmann arose not from naturalism or realism but from an overriding spiritual ethos, godly in those earlier painters, demonic and distraught in his work. Every element was to have its claim of fascination on the eye of the viewer, bringing all sensation and intelligence to the same tormented emotional level. In this sense, the abolishment of perspective was an ur-political gesture. It refused conventional orders or hierarchies of morality in order to depict the ramifications of "murderousness" as an ongoing state of affairs. Beckmann's condition as a "loner," even within the tradition of German Expressionism to which the critics allied him, was now a stance outside of a stance.

Kentridge, in his essay, notes that *Tot* depicts "the world as contested arena." As we are pulled into its dislocating fervor, not only do we experience the dizzying pain and alienation of its creator, but we also find ourselves at that psychological threshold where our objective reality suddenly seems vertiginous. Some great paintings enthrall, but this one by Beckmann, even as it captivates, also throws its viewers into emotional and ethical uncertainty. *Tot* is a powerful painting but also a great and threatening critique of the world.

We could ponder that the "Western gaze," that act/anti-act of contemplation as epitomized at its extreme in the painterly meditations on death in Velásquez and Manet, is actually a realm of absorption from which objectivity and reason have been banished. A true critique of the gaze—the gaze we all participate in—would underline its falsehood. For it is a site "outside" so to speak, disguising or hiding our instinctual, mostly infantile drives that have no part in morality or ethics but are consumed in brute fear, greed and violence. Beckmann's *Tot* forces us out of that gaze as few works do, back into the actual life we are leading.

OTHER POEMS

MOTHER ASLEEP

after a painting by Leon Kossoff

What if the mother
      is always sick,
what if for her whole life,
      she is sick

—when we were children—
      weren't we
always asking: is that sleep
      she is sleeping

or is it a slide toward death?
      What is it
to be always in fear,
      isn't that ridiculous,

that one's hug
      or one's moving too near
could hurt?
      Isn't that *hurtful?*

Don't these thoughts
          pend on a life
like a painter's heavy impasto?
          Don't they distort

what he paints,
          bending it from one
understandable realm
          into the fearful next?

Seeing her in the chair,
          her head atilt,
or lying on her bed,
          the child's eye

inevitably trailed
          away from her being there,
followed the lines
          formed by the drapery of sheets

or by the downward flow
          of hidden limbs,
—gravity pulled at the eye
          and fated it.

And isn't this why
          Kossoff painted
a bright red blotch
          just below his mother's left hand

—nothing structural
          in its being there
—nothing in the image
          or design to fix it,

—*red blot*
  of a child's anger—
formless,
  homeless—

didn't it wander
  like a loose speck,
like an errant cyst
  in a teary eye?

Notes: R.B. Kitaj at Marlborough

Do for Jews what Morandi did for jars . . .
—Second Diasporist Manifesto, RBK

'small' pictures, dull brown canvas,
rills of paint—bravura strokes

petering out

luminosity had been his fame
—now subdued, brushed lines muted,

ghosted as were his Jewish ghosts
his beloved Scholem, a wrinkled tilted egg.

Arendt's face pressed against a green
vertical, one eye blocked

Jerusalem!

what, for him, did her acuity miss: Heidegger
or *Shoah*'s horrors, vast beyond banality?

he's Kafka's Gregor on his back with questions,
Sandra *Shekinah* gone, *gone*, but still, in loving

paint the daubs float on thick fibre
"leaving," "gone," the words punctuate

his second manifesto, death as a "Jewish Question"?
impossibility of a breakthrough, of an answer

to.

WITHIN THE OPEN LANDSCAPES

words for the etchings of Jane Joseph

1. Doesn't the picture say
no room in this world for anything more?
If you desire to add something,
you must begin again
and make your own world,
including what has been missing
from the very beginning
of the world.

You must make an enormous effort
to leave this world for that one,
something like dying, if not quite.

Each world is so complete,
terror and emptiness
accompany every effort to leave it.

2. Black parts of things
keep the eye centered on the dark.
At least one can see
a bit of upstanding twig
leads to the branch,
leads along the branch
until the branch
foregrounded before flowing water
invites a sojourn past woods and house
along its banks.

Clouds are always on the move,
and suggest the weather's alterations.
Darks do no more than keep the eye
centered on the dark.

3. When the things of the world
are so carefully depicted
—when we see such things—
surely we surrender a little, giving
ourselves over to the thing seen.

I have heard others speaking
of the tree's *treeness*
or an object's *being*.
I have looked,
and each time I experience something
—my own disappearance,
my own failed going-out
to meet the tree,
to meet the object.

Nothing coming back.

4. I can love a picture
but only if it doesn't love me.
I insist on boundaries.
I can hate a picture
without it hating me.
I don't insist on boundaries.

5. The branch of the sycamore
forks two ways,
one limb sort of down
and flat across the paper,
the other making an upthrust
so powerful it begins
to curve back on itself
as though the light was the light
of a nourishing self-regard
and the wide-spaced faint scribble
marks that go near the vertical
were the accidental pleas of space itself
warning against hubris.

6. So many bridges, foot, railway, auto,
each obscured by the surrounding designs,
are mythologies of difficult contact.
Or child's stories where ogres
are secreted in dark patches under pathways
by which we connect.

7. The daffodil hangs its heavy blossomed head.
Wordsworth has shamed you.
And Eliot made the hyacinth

the flower of rebirth
into death's blossoming

You are lone upon the heath.
You are between realms,
between cliché and astonishment.

8. And let the picture transform you.
Let this thistle put on its fiery fall color,
and let its bunched tufts
resemble a wrathful deity,
and let the corolla be a necklace
of enlaced skulls, and let homage be paid
by the ground underfoot,
its otherness crushing
ego's unreasonable hectorings,
and let the mind never rest
in the false nirvana of vegetative happiness,
and let the bumble bee alight,
thick-dusted with the pollen of awareness.

CAPRICCIO WITH OBELISK

Bowes Museum, Barnard Castle

We followed the pictures,
and the pictures followed us

the way religion follows a soul
and tries to contain it.

Did the one who suffered
come into a place

where a thing belonged neither
to Caesar nor the Sanhedrin?

Not the physical object itself
but what it gave off

or what it meant to us,
and why therefore

someone owned it.

Was there, in that martyred life,
some surcease, some pause?

And earlier, did Socrates
admire the hemlock-filled cup?

Why did we stand
before the firestorm in Tiepolo,

seeing it burst over worked-in horses,
chariots and reins   clouds scattered—

no, shattered—by light from the sun?
How did others' immense suffering

tutor us—those blinding rays
that streamed as background

to the picture's paraphernalia,
illuminating our blessings?

Was it knowledge of an illusion?
Those who made art

in the death camps, only to die
—what did they leave us?

So much were we given:
the obelisk in the faux garden,

an amusement, a painter's
whim of juxtaposition?

We were being given artifice
and asked to embrace it.

Thus, the life-sized swan-clock
in the glass case carried

implications of destiny
but was also a joke,

its hammered plates "afloat"
on watery ribbons of silvered metal.

A key was turned, sound
came out as from an organ

and the space was "filled
with Mechanism beating Time

with its beak to musical chimes . . ."
The whole shimmered

and all clapped hands at the ingenuity.

And nearby, Goya's *Interior of a Prison*
lay somber and flat,

a series of increasingly diminished arches,
light darkening as the eye followed curves

back to where Time had stopped beating,
to where Time was not.

And so the images followed us
with their baggage and hope.

The graven became sacred,
became as a shelter

—the man on the cross
and the Jew in the pit—

these were given as ours to contain us
in paradise and in dungeons.

Lightning Source UK Ltd.
Milton Keynes UK
06 March 2010

151030UK00001B/6/P

9 781848 610873